CONTENTS

D1176187

FeeL THE POWER!

The Gogo's now have more energy than ever, more power, new skills and abilities.

Get to know your new Gogo's and prepare to enter the world of Power Gogo's!

01 POWI

POWER

Well connected and very popular. This Gogo is always sending messages to friends.

POWER SYMBOL

All Gogo's have one of three different power symbols; ray, star and spiral. These provide each Gogo with special capabilities.

NAME AND NUMBER

Every Gogo has a name and number. You'll find all their names in this handbook. If you look closely at the back of your Gogo, you'll find its number printed just above the MAGIC BOX INT. stamp.

GOGO PERSONALITIES

Each Gogo is very special and has its own personality and special abilities. If you want to know more about them, you can read their profiles right here in this handbook. You'll also find information on each of the Gogo's favourite games.

01 POWI

POWER

Well connected and very popular. This Gogo is always sending messages to friends.

MOST WANTED

You can recognize the MOST WANTED Gogo's by this symbol.

HOW TO PLAY?

You'll never be bored with a Gogo; so many games to play including the exciting new card games! Different Gogo's are better for playing different games depending on their size, shape and weight. Check out the profiles and use the handy guide to find out which games will best suit your Gogo's.

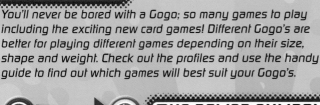

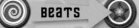

THE POWER SYMBOLS

The ray, the star and the spiral are three great powers that provide each Gogo with special capabilities. You can use these when playing the card games to find out who beats who and who is the winner!

If both cards have the same symbol, there is a tie.

On the back of each card you will find this graphic to remind you which card beats the other.

COLOURS

Each Gogo is available in four different colours. All the colours of every Gogo can be found at the back of this handbook in the checklist section.

THE BACK

Look on the back of your Gogo's and you'll find they are all designed the same so that you can hold them or throw them with just one finger. Of course, practice is the key to becoming a Gogo champion.

DON'T ACCEPT IMITATIONS

Pick up a Gogo and turn it over to check that it has the MAGIC BOX INT. stamp. The MAGIC BOX INT. stamp guarantees that your Gogo is an original, has a fantastic bounce and is a bright, shiny colour.

TRADING CARD GAME!

You are probably wondering what you have to do with those wonderful new cards you got with your latest Power Gogo's. Have no fear! The Gogo experts are here to guide you through the exciting new game.

PLAYING THE GAME

1 Each player draws four cards from their collection without letting the other player see the front of them or the power logo on the back of their game cards.

2 Choose one of these cards to be your knockout card. Both players place their knockout card on the table at the same time with the power logo showing and at an agreed distance from each other. Place the Gogo shown on the face of the card on top of your knockout card.

3 At exactly the same time, both players throw down one of their three remaining Power cards.

4 Compare the power symbols on facing cards. Use the chart on page 3 of this handbook to tell you which symbol beats another. Award players a point for every win. If both cards have the same symbol the point is tied.

5 The player with the most points wins. However, there is a chance for the losing player to win the game outright by a knockout. This can ONLY happen if their third power card beats their opponent's and the symbol matches the symbol on their opponent's knockout card.

MATCHING SYMBOLS

6 Then they can take a knockout shot. The losing player must flick their Gogo to try and knock their opponent's Gogo off their card. Knocking an opponent's Gogo over wins the match outright.

MAGIC MAZE!

Tachan loves his magic tricks but is also extremely forgetful when it comes to keeping his hands on his equipment.

Can you help him get hold of all his stuff before he has to put on a show for the rest of the Gogo's?

FINISH

START

FINISH

FINISH

FIND ALL THE ANSWERS ON PAGE 88

HAMO'S TIDY UP!

Hamo just can't stand mess. Can you follow the lines and help him return all the items to the Gogo's who have left them lying around?

01 POWI ♂

POWER

Well connected and very popular. This Gogo is always sending messages to friends.

02 HIK ♂

POWER

Even with more than twenty special fighting moves, Hik uses his head first.

PROFILES

03   eRYU

POWER

This Gogo is trying to use war paint to help win some games. Could it work?

04   CORa

POWER

Cora can hear the music of the sea and can sing with the most perfect voice.

05 WELU

POWER

Welu can jump from one planet to another... provided he doesn't lose his mask.

06 GEON

POWER

A mean face and a special helmet... always ready for the worst!

PROFILES

07 MINDOK

POWER

The most honourable
Gogo of them all,
Mindok could never cheat.

08 SINI

POWER

Her mysterious face hides
a power that nobody has
ever discovered.

09 KIU-SUN

POWER

A Gogo with solar power?
That is Xiu-Sun.

10 HORO

POWER

One, two, three... Horo is gone!
A quick thinking Gogo.

PROFILES

11 OKIIMO

POWER

Tries to be early but always arrives late.

12 ASDARIN

POWER

Everyone knows that Asdarin controls a great magical mystery.

FUN-TIME FRENZY!

FOROLIN'S

With the ability to fly anywhere, Forolin has travelled the world many times. He loves the shapes of different countries and their colourful flags.

FLIGHTS OF FANCY!

Can you identify all the countries – and their flags – that Forolin has visited? Forolin bets you can't.

FIND ALL THE ANSWERS ON PAGE 88

CROSSED WORDS!

Think you have the power? Are you an expert on Eryu? A genius on Geon? Now is your chance to prove your skills.

All the answers can be found in this book so get your thinking cap on and unleash the power.

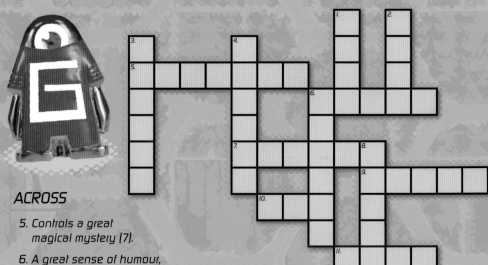

ACROSS

5. Controls a great magical mystery (7).

6. A great sense of humour, for a robot (5).

7. What type of professional is Poto? (6).

9. Changes costumes every week and might be useful as a toothpaste (5).

10. His giant eye does all the work (3).

11. If you needed a unique Gogo alloy who would you talk to? (4).

DOWN

1. If you needed to send a message which Gogo would be most helpful? (4).

2. A real expert at demolition (4).

3. Silien has a special power, what is it? (7).

4. Solid as a rock, but can you rearrange OARNCB to find out who it is. (7).

6. His name rhymes with ketchup who is he? (7).

8. What does Flek use to invite everyone to play? (7).

FIND ALL THE ANSWERS ON PAGE 89

JIGSAW JUMBLE!

After working together on a jigsaw, the Gogo's have left everything in a mess! Help Binlod use his mechanical visual system to finish off the jigsaw.

a

B

C

D

 F

 e

G

17

PROFILES

13 DOSK

POWER

Scary to look at
but underneath is a
heart of gold.

14 TERIN

POWER

Sometimes Terin thinks all his
friends have run away.... but
they are right in front of him!

PROFILES

15 SHOD

POWER

Five super-fast teeth make quick work of every meal! Never shares food with anyone.

16 DUMIEL

POWER

A friend to nature and always to be found exploring the forest.

17 REYU

POWER

A master at hiding low down and popping up to surprise the others.

18 SILIEN

POWER

A unique robot with vacuum power. No corner is left untouched.

19 BILA

POWER

Uses special antennae to detect hidden sweets.

20 GAT

POWER

Gat absorbs all the heat and energy from the air and recycles it for his friends.

21 MOOR

POWER

With half a face hidden, this Gogo isn't easy to read. No one likes to guess what Moor is thinking.

22 KILO

POWER

An unusual power surrounds Kilo, something that makes everyone want to look his way.

23 WAWO

POWER

A Gogo sage who can guide the others in important matters.

24 HAMO

POWER

A reputation for being messy and dirty, but is actually obsessed with being clean.

IN-PO'S TRIVIA

1 What is wrong with this picture of Irgo?

A. Too many eyes ☐

B. Wrong shape ☐

C. Missing star logo ☐

2 I have a super brain to help keep up with my super-fast body. Who am I?

A. Jaki ☐

B. Horo-W ☐

C. Fil Dan ☐

3 Which Gogo is the king of spirals?

A. Ruyt ☐

B. Geon ☐

C. Woki ☐

4  Which Gogo proudly sports this logo?

☐

5 Can you re-arrange these letters to give you the name of a Gogo?

(A) (H) (C) (T) (N) (A)

☐ ☐ ☐ ☐ ☐ ☐

FIND ALL THE ANSWERS ON PAGE 90

FUN-TIME FRENZY!

GOGO® PILE-UP!

The Gogo factory machines have got out of control again. Can you help by counting up how many of each Gogo you can see and entering the numbers in the boxes below?

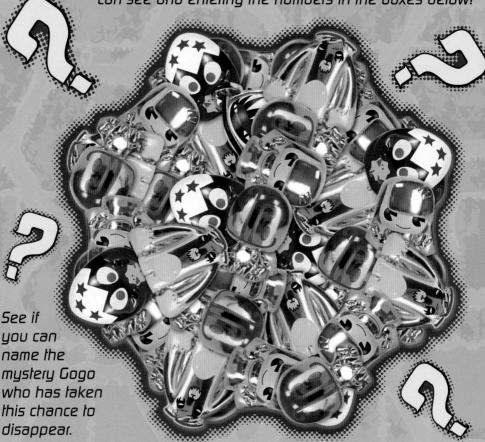

See if you can name the mystery Gogo who has taken this chance to disappear.

MYSTERY GOGO!

FIND ALL THE ANSWERS ON PAGE 90

SKIMO's SEARCH

Can you help Skimo find all the Power Gogo's that are hiding in his igloo?

Use the list below to help you find all the Power Gogo's names.

```
                  G N Y Z
        A S O K R O D R K O
        W N A P I R E V Z A X T
      S F A K L N X Z I E K U W E
    H D A M W I A L K N N O Y R A M
  A G V O N R O J C H E L O H D O D Y
  F U H J A R A E B I N I O L O R I T
  U O I U V P A N O L O O N Y H A W R V N
W B R K G N K O O S O I D G I R A D S A O U F
A A S D A R I N S Y S I O P Z C O R O D A N N
W B O L T Z R N F H G M I O G O Q U J F X I P O
F U G Q R J Q R V J O W D F E T U Y P X F U S A R
Z Q H X O E B A D Q D D M F O U I T E X P F Q R L
S H C O N R A B G W H P C L N F S X Z D A R K L
```

- ASDARIN
- BABU
- CONRAB
- DIRO
- ERHON
- FUSA
- GEON
- GUIN
- KAKO
- REIN
- RUYT
- SHOD
- SILIEN
- VARIN
- WAWO

27

FIND ALL THE ANSWERS ON PAGE 91

25 IRGO

POWER

A demolition expert. Nothing is an obstacle.

26 SHAWA

POWER

Shawa can see your ancestors whilst dreaming. An interesting Gogo to know.

27 BABU

POWER

Shy Babu will never push forward to the front.

28 JAHI

POWER

Loves nothing more than to win by K.O. That's what the bumper helmet is designed for.

29 DAK

POWER

Dak listens to music all day long. He loves to dance!

30 TEGO

POWER

Made from a unique Gogo alloy, Tego's body can bend in an unusual way.

PROFILES

POWER 9090'S
CRAZY BONES

31 DIN

POWER

Not easy to find
but if you do, Din may
grant you a wish...

32 FICHUP

POWER

A salsa-dancing expert
who just loves to shake
his bones.

POWER 9090's CRAZY BONES

PROFILES

33 MOODEL

POWER

Cuddly and adorable, everyone wants to hold Moodel in their arms.

34 GARIN

POWER

The light that enters through his eyes, fills him with energy.

PROFILES

35 FIVOK ♂

POWER

The only robot we know with a great sense of humour.

36 KAKO

POWER

At night,
Kako can move around
without being seen.

FUN-TIME FRENZY!

GOGO® DOODLE!

Drawing a Gogo can be straightforward but everyone needs a hand now and again.

Use the image of the Gogo in the grid to transfer it to the larger grid. Don't forget that every Gogo needs to be as colourful as possible so get your colouring pens out.

SINI

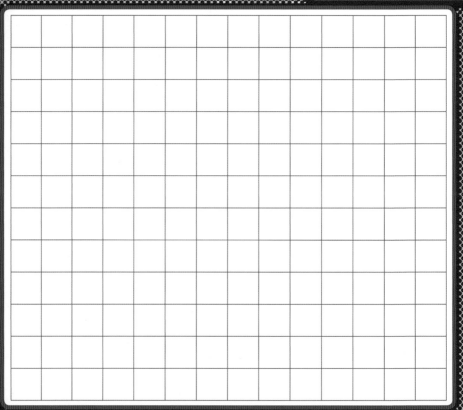

GOGO DOODLE!

FUN-TIME FRENZY!

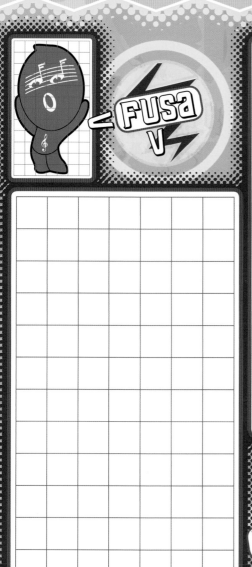

FUSA
v

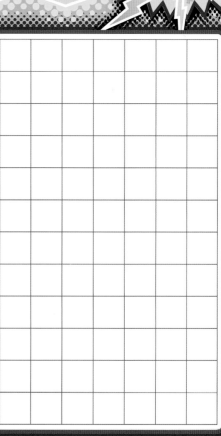

VARIN RAY

GAME RULES

online

1 Use any line on the ground or draw one yourself. Each player throws a Gogo without dragging it.

2 The player who manages to throw their Gogo nearest the line wins the throw.

3 If a player manages to get a Gogo directly on the line they score double points.

4 The player who wins the most throws wins the game.

GAME RULES

BATTLE

1 Two players arrange six or more of their Gogo's in parallel rows a short distance apart.

2 Players must decide before the start of the match how many throws there will be.

3 Players then throw their Gogo at their opponent's row and attempt to knock Gogo's out of the line.

4 The player who knocks down the most of their opponent's Gogo's wins.

TIPS

If using basic rules, the Gogo's do not need to fall over completely, but simply be knocked out of the line.

If you want to play advanced rules, then the Gogo's must actually be knocked over as well as being pushed out of the line.

PROFILES

37 FLEK

POWER

Flek has a smile that invites everyone to play.

38 RITA

POWER

After escaping from a top-secret lab, Rita hides day and night, just in case...

39 ZaPPI

POWER

Anti-shock armour and diving skills give this Gogo a lot of advantages.

40 FRUG

POWER

Somehow Frug is first and last in everything. Not even he knows how he does it!

91 SKIIMO

POWER

Able to handle the coldest climate with ultra-warm clothing power.

92 YUTO

POWER

A good friend of Hik, he's taller and stronger, though less agile.

PROFILES

43 FIL DAN

POWER

A terrifying laugh makes the other Gogo's nervous. Should they be?

44 GULFRED

POWER

Probably the hairiest Gogo of them all. Nobody feels like combing him.

95 ERHON

POWER

Put Erhon together with Irgo and they could split just about anything.

96 BELION

POWER

The sun and the stars grant him a lion's strength.

PROFILES

47 EUL

POWER

Behind these looks is a weightlifting champion.

48 UYU

POWER

A giant eye that can see all angles. The body doesn't move but the eye rotates!

WAR PAINT

Eryu never goes into a game without his war paint. Unfortunately, all that playing doesn't give him much time to work on new and interesting looks for his game-winning technique.

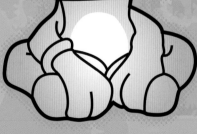

WORKSHOP!

Can you help Eryu out by getting your colouring pens and designing him some new looks? You can make them scary, pretty or whatever you want. Remember the more colourful the better.

FUN-TIME FRENZY!

MOOR'S THOUGHTS!

The other Gogo's always find it difficult to guess what Moor is thinking. Can you help them out by taking a look into Moor's mind and letting the Gogo's know exactly what objects he is thinking about?

FIND ALL THE ANSWERS ON PAGE 91

IN-PO'S TRIVIA

1 Can you name which two Gogo's have got a little mixed-up here?

3 How many spots make up Vlio's sun logo?

4 Which game would you be playing if you managed to get double points for landing directly on a line?

5 What is wrong with this picture of Vite?

2 If you take Terin's number away from Varin Ray's number which number and Gogo will you have?

A. 49 Taku ⭕

B. 10 Horo ⭕

C. 78 Fenton ⭕

47

FIND ALL THE ANSWERS ON PAGE 92

49 TAKU

POWER

A skilful night-time flyer who watches over the other Gogo's.

50 HIID

POWER

Moves quickly in and out of busy traffic and keeps things moving.

PROFILES

S1 LIM

POWER

Lim has the ability to turn an enemy into a friend within moments.

S2 LULO

POWER

The roundest Gogo of them all. Moves with speed and skill using protected eyes.

S3 GOOMI

POWER

He can change the colour of his body, but don't ask him to change his T-shirt.

S4 WOHI

POWER

Considering he is the king of spirals, he looks fairly harmless.

PROFILES

S5 BRANCO

POWER

He is as solid as a rock. Many have tried to move him and many have failed.

S6 FUSA

POWER

A musical genius who can control the power of echoes.

PROFILES

S7 FOROLIN

POWER

Go here, go there,
Forolin flies anywhere.

S8 BINLOD

POWER

A mechanical visual system
allows him to calculate the
size of everything he sees.

PROFILES

59 CONRAB

POWER

Brings good luck to all
the Gogo's, just as long as
things go his way...

60 GI-KAO

POWER

Gives out a crazy shriek
before each strike – Gi-Kao!

GAME RULES

K.O.

1 Using a piece of chalk, mark a square (or circle) on the floor.

2 Each player must place the same number of Gogo's inside the square. Decide on the number of throws each player will get.

3 Players take turns to stand two metres away and throw a Gogo into the square in an attempt to knock their opponent's Gogo's out of the square.

K.O.

4 If a Gogo gets knocked over but not completely out of the square, it can be put back into position, even if it falls on the line.

5 The winner is the player with the most Gogo's left in the square at the end of the agreed number of throws.

GAME RULES

SCORING

1 Players choose the number of Gogo's to be used. This can be anything from one to five Gogo's at a time.

2 Each player takes turns to throw their Gogo's on the floor.

POWER a-GOGO!

3 Using the chart below, work out your score by looking at how the Gogo's land.

4 Each player has three goes and the one with the highest score at the end wins. Of course, you can take more turns if you are looking for a longer game!

SCORE CHART

| 5 POINTS | 2 POINTS | 1 POINTS | 0 POINTS |

ALMO'S AMAZING

Almo is obsessed by fashion and it just drives this poor Gogo mad that Goomi will never change his T-shirt.

In an attempt to make Goomi look more fabulous, Almo needs your help to design some amazing new shirts. Go crazy with your colours or make him look dark and cool – it's up to you. Just remember, it has to be fabulous and fashionable to impress Almo.

T-SHIRT SHOP!

FUN-TIME FRENZY!

WELU'S STARGAZING!

While Welu spends a lot of his time jumping from planet to planet he sees some amazing sights out in the depths of the universe.

Join the dots to see his latest discovery, don't forget you can colour it in too.

GARIN'S SPOT-IT!

With his energy-filled eye there isn't much that Garin misses. When taking a recent photo of the Gogo's he's sure there is something wrong.

Can you help Garin out by spotting the 10 differences between these two pictures. Make sure you find them all or the other Gogo's will make fun of Garin for a long time.

59

FIND ALL THE ANSWERS ON PAGE 92

61 KUSTOR

POWER

Kustor plays all day and rides his motorbike all night.

62 URKII

POWER

Happy to be a loyal pet but you should never tie him up and leave him alone.

PROFILES

63 POTO ♂

POWER

A circus professional who is always making the other Gogo's laugh.

64 VARIN RAY ♂

POWER

The chief of security whenever the Power Gogo's get together.

PROFILES

65 VLIO

POWER

Vlio and Cora are
great friends and share
a love for the sea.

66 FRISPIRICANDY

POWER

The sweetest of Gogo's
and one that sends Bila's
antennae crazy!

PROFILES

67 ## GUIN

POWER

A super-cool Gogo that can swim in the coldest water of all.

68 ## ILO

POWER

Is this a Gogo tortoise looking for a missing shell?

PROFILES

69 VITE

POWER

The slightest movement in the distance activates his detection device.

70 DODA

POWER

That head is square from watching too much TV.

PROFILES

POWER GOGO'S
CRAZY BONES

71 IN-PO

POWER

The guide to all questions that you may have about Power Gogo's.

72 RUYT

POWER

Ruyt can get things a little confused sometimes but gets there in the end.

DIRO-W'S ST3

To become a member of the Most Wanted
Power Gogo's takes some pretty amazing skills.
Diro-W has asked if you can help him sort out
the latest batch of potential recruits.

You can use any colour you want and see if you can find out just

aLTH SCHOOL!

Some of the Gogo's have been given the task of blending into the surroundings as well as Diro-W does himself. Can you reveal them by colouring in only the shapes that have dots in them?

which Gogo's are trying to make it into the Most Wanted group.

FUN-TIME FRENZY!

DESIGN A GOGO®!

By now you must be itching to have a go at making your own Gogo. Use the outlines we've given you here and make your own Gogo design.

Remember you can be as colourful as you like and add any designs you want. Don't forget to give them a name!

DESIGN A GUGU®!

73 TACHAN

POWER

An apprentice magician who very often forgets to bring a wand.

74 ALMO

POWER

Fashion is everything to this Gogo. Nobody has more wardrobes.

PROFILES

75 DIRO

POWER

Stays bright and happy, even without sleep for three days.

76 ERENDEL

POWER

Can often be found hiding in the hollow of a tree, ready to surprise Dumiel.

PROFILES

77 SPIR

POWER

With ticklish feet Spir would love to find some shoes that fit.

78 FENTON

POWER

Not all Gogo's believe it but Fenton can fly to the moon.

79 MINTY

POWER

Changes costumes each week.
Other Gogo's guess what
will be next.

80 REIN

POWER

Rein has an ability to
detect secret underground
water sources.

IN-PO'S TRIVIA

1 If you needed a lift on a motorbike at night, which Gogo should you call?

A. Almo ☐

B. Gat ☐

C. Kustor ☐

2 Can you guess which out of focus Gogo this is?

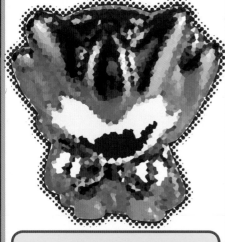

3 If you were looking into this eye which Gogo would you be face to face with?

4 Which Gogo should you never tie up and leave alone?

5 Take Zappi's Gogo number and add 7. Take away 20. Add 44 and which Gogo do you end up with?

A. 70 Doda ☐

B. 47 Eul ☐

C. 08 Sini ☐

FIND ALL THE ANSWERS ON PAGE 93

BILA'S SWEET SEARCH!

Bila's amazing ability to detect sweets doesn't always work. Can you help find the hidden stash of sweets by using the map and directions below?

From the START:

1. Travel north to the anchor.
2. Travel five paces east.
3. Walk three paces south.
4. Travel east to the ship's wheel.
5. Head north two paces.
6. Trek west for seven paces.
7. Walk four paces south.
8. Mark the spot with an X!

75

FIND ALL THE ANSWERS ON PAGE 93

05 WELU-W

POWER

Added power for reaching the farthest galaxies.

10 HORO-W

POWER

A super brain and a super-fast body.

POWER GOGO'S CRAZY BONES!

20 GaT-W

POWER

Creates a ray of light to guide all the other Gogo's.

30 TEGO-W

POWER

Can this metal sensor unlock secret powers?

90 FRUG-W

POWER

What came first, the chicken or the scrambled egg?

50 HIIID-W

POWER

Communicates important information through the air.

60 GI-KAO-W

POWER

Gi-Kao power helps to make every K.O. shot a winner.

70 DODA-W

POWER

Uses positive TV powers to turn into a TV superhero!

75 DIRO-W

W

POWER

Adapts to the surroundings with colour-changing power.

80 REIN-W

W

POWER

Uses green power to pump water to the others.

CHECKLIST

Have you got all the Gogo's? This is a list of all the Power Gogo's Crazy Bones® available. Use it to keep track of the ones you've got and the ones you still need to collect.

01 POWI

02 HIK

03 ERYU

04 CORA

05 WELU

06 GEON

07 MINDOK

08 SINI

09 KIU-SUN

10 HORO

39 ZAPPI

90 FRUG

91 SKIMO

92 YUTO

93 FIL DAN

99 GULFRED

95 ERHON

96 BELION

97 EUL

98 UYU

99 TAKU

50 HIID

51 LIM

52 LULU

 53 GOOMI

 54 WOKI

 55 BRANCO

 56 FUSA

 57 FOROLIN

 58 BINLOD

 59 CONRAB

 60 GI-KAO

 61 KUSTOR

 62 URKI

 63 POTO

 64 VARIN RAY

 65 VLIO

 66 FRISPIRICANDY

67 GUIN

68 ILO

69 VITE

70 DODA + 70 W

71 IN-PO

72 RUYT

73 TACHAN

74 ALMO

75 DIRO + 75 W

76 ERENDEL

77 SPIR

78 FENTON

79 MINTY

80 REIN + 80 W

ANSWERS — ANSWERS!

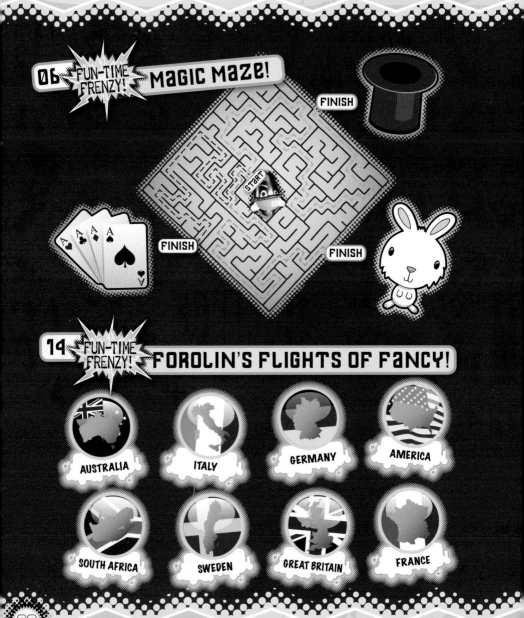

06 FUN-TIME FRENZY! **MAGIC MAZE!**

FINISH

START

FINISH

FINISH

14 FUN-TIME FRENZY! **FOROLIN'S FLIGHTS OF FANCY!**

AUSTRALIA

ITALY

GERMANY

AMERICA

SOUTH AFRICA

SWEDEN

GREAT BRITAIN

FRANCE

16 FUN-TIME FRENZY! **CROSSED WORDS!**

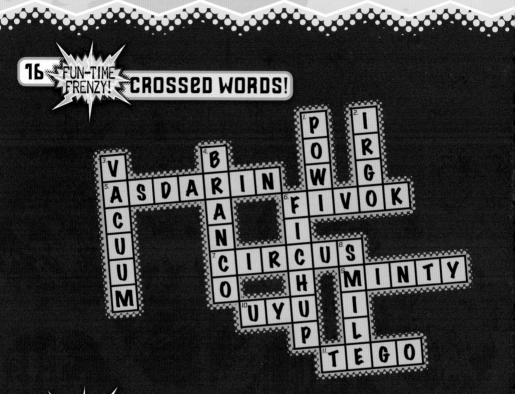

17 FUN-TIME FRENZY! **JIGSAW JUMBLE!**

D

F

G

ANSWERS-ANSWERS!

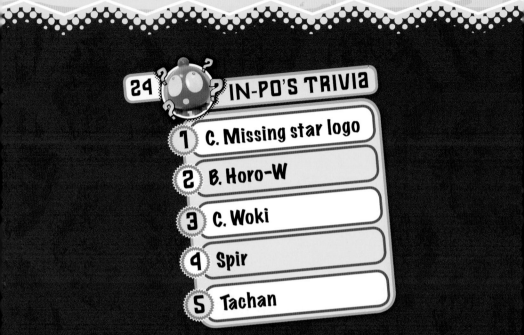

24 IN-PO'S TRIVIA

1. C. Missing star logo
2. B. Horo-W
3. C. Woki
4. Spir
5. Tachan

26 FUN-TIME FRENZY! GOGO PILE UP!

 8   6   13   10

MYSTERY GOGO!  Eul

ANSWERS – ANSWERS!

27 FUN-TIME FRENZY! SKIMO'S SEARCH

96 FUN-TIME FRENZY! MOOR'S THOUGHTS!

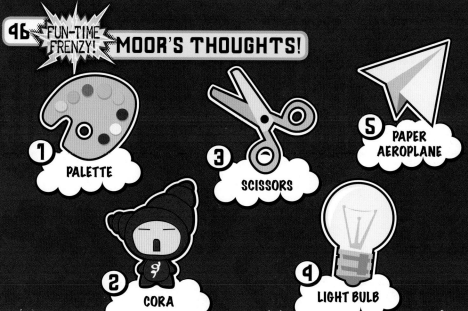

1 PALETTE

2 CORA

3 SCISSORS

4 LIGHT BULB

5 PAPER AEROPLANE

ANSWERS — ANSWERS!

47 IN-PO'S TRIVIA

1 Minty & Doda-W

2 A. 49

3 Seven

4 On-line

5 Wrong colour goggles

59 FUN-TIME FRENZY! GARIN'S SPOT-IT!

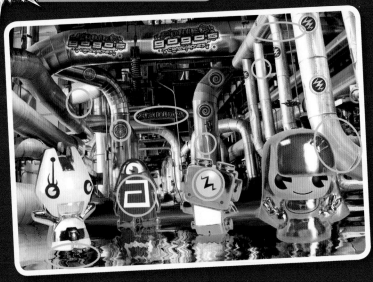

ANSWERS – ANSWERS!

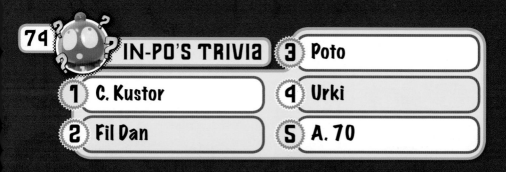

74 **IN-PO'S TRIVIA**

1 C. Kustor

2 Fil Dan

3 Poto

4 Urki

5 A. 70

75 FUN-TIME FRENZY! **BILA'S SWEET SEARCH!**

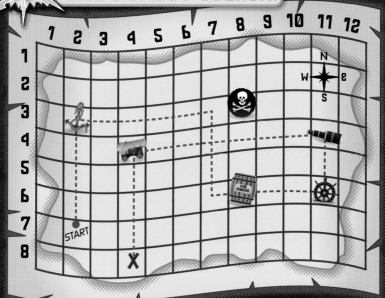

POWER GOGO'S
CRAZY BONES
Official
HANDBOOK

GOGO'S CRAZY BONES ® POWER GOGO'S OFFICIAL HANDBOOK
A BANTAM BOOK 978 0 553 82217 5
First published in Great Britain by Bantam
an imprint of Random House Children's Books
A Random House Group Company
This edition published 2009
1 2 3 4 5 6 7 8 9 10
GOGO'S/CRAZY BONES © 2009 PPI – MARTOMAGIC, S.L.U.
All rights reserved
Bantam Books are published by Random House Children's Books,
61-63 Uxbridge Road, London W5 5SA
www.**rbooks**.co.uk
www.**kidsatrandomhouse**.co.uk
Addresses for companies within The Random house Group Limited can be found at:
www.randomhouse.co.uk/offices.htm
THE RANDOM HOUSE GROUP Limited Reg. No. 954009
A CIP catalogue record for this book is available from the British Library
Printed in Italy

MAGIC BOX INT.®

ppi Worldwide